WORLD FOLKTALES

A Multicultural Approach to Whole Language

GRADES 3–5

By Jerry Mallett
and
Keith Polette

Alleyside Press

Fort Atkinson, Wisconsin

Published by Alleyside Press, an imprint of Highsmith Press
Highsmith Press
W5527 Highway 106
P.O. Box 800
Fort Atkinson, Wisconsin 53538-0800

1-800-558-2110

© Jerry Mallett and Keith Polette, 1994
Cover design: Frank Neu

The paper used in this publication meets the minimum requirements of
American National Standard for Information Science —
Permanence of Paper for Printed Library Material. ANSI/NISO Z39.48-1992.

Library of Congress Cataloging in Publication
   Mallet, Jerry J., 1939-
      World folktales : a multicultural approach to whole language /
   by Jerry Mallett and Keith Polette.
         p.   cm.
      Includes bibliographical references.
      Contents: [1] K-2 -- [2] 3-5 -- [3] 6-8.
      ISBN 0-917846-43-5 (v. 1 : alk. paper). --ISBN 0-917846-44-3
      (v. 2 : alk. paper). -- ISBN 0-917846-45-1 (v. 3 : alk. paper)
       1. Tales--Study and teaching (Elementary)--United States.
      2. Language experience approach in education--United States.
      3. Multicultural education--United States.
      I. Polette, Keith, 1954-   . II. Title.
      LB1576.M3625 1994
      372.64--dc20   94-21691

CONTENTS

INTRODUCTION

This book is based upon the premise that children learn most effectively and efficiently by becoming active participants in the process of education. Quite simply, this means that children learn least when they sit passively for hours and read and respond to material in which they are not both mentally and emotionally engaged. One approach which allows and encourages children to become more involved in learning is Whole Language. Whole Language is not a system, or a specific set of strategies, but is rather a different kind of educational orientation which places the student at the center of the learning situation. Consequently, Whole Language relies heavily upon the perceptions and experiences that the student brings to the classroom every day because these experiences are the base upon which Whole Language is built.

The activities in *World Folktales: A Multicultural Approach to Whole Language*, are designed to help the teacher create a Whole Language environment by using the experiences of the student as a bridge to increased literacy through active involvement. In addition, the activities are holistic in format, being based as they are upon a multiplicity of both productive and critical (higher order) thinking skills, which means that the whole student, not just an isolated part of his/her brain, will be engaged in learning.

The specific educational objectives of this book are for the student to: gain an appreciation for folktales as a literary genre; gain an increased understanding and appreciation of world cultures as expressed through their various folktales; demonstrate high order thinking processes with increased facility; acquire a higher level of literacy; develop more efficient writing, speaking and listening skills; develop the ability to respond to a literary text in a myriad of clear and purposeful ways; develop more sophisticated language patterns; and develop a strong working vocabulary.

The activities in this book are ready to be used in the language arts classroom without requiring a great deal of preparation time. Many are also designed to be enjoyable, to take the malaise that many students feel out of learning. Consequently, this book will help the teacher create a strong sense of "psychological safety" in the classroom. When students feel "safe," that is, when they feel that their experiences, perceptions and ideas are valid and acceptable, they will often see more purpose for reading, writing, speaking, listening and thinking in the classroom. The Whole Language approach allows the teacher to become more of a facilitator and to also make his/her job easier and more rewarding. When both the students and the teacher are relaxed, true learning begins.

BOOK ORGANIZATION

For easy use and clarity, *World Folktales: A Multicultural Approach to Whole Language* is arranged into the following eight cultural units:

West European (Sweden)

Asian (Japan)

African American/Africa (Ethiopia)

American Indian/Inuit (Canadian Indian)

Hispanic (Costa Rica)

Middle East/India (Arabian)

Jewish/Yiddish

East European (Russia)

These eight cultural sections are organized into uniform units. Each unit begins with a folktale indigenous to that particular cultural group. This is followed by three activity sections emphasizing the Whole-Language approach: Before Reading Activities, During Reading Activities and After Reading Activities. Each unit is completed with student activity sheets which may be copied for immediate student use.

A "Story Integration" section may be found at the end of the book. This section is composed of Whole-Language activities which overlap and combine all of the folktales found here.

THE SECRET INGREDIENT
FOLKTALE FROM SWEDEN

Early one fall, a stranger entered the village of Luphen. He was tall and thin as a cedar sapling. His cloths hung on him like rags on a stick. The villagers, who had gathered in the square to watch him, eyed him warily for they had nothing to spare for a hungry beggar. Their eyes grew as wide as soup bowls as they watched him sit down and take something out of his pocket. Clenching the mysterious object between both hands, he made slow circular motions with his fists locked together.

An old woman shouted at the stranger, "What are you doing?"

Without looking up, the stranger said, "I'm making my lunch," and continued to stir the air.

The old woman said, "Lunch! Hunger must have made you daft, man. There's no food here."

For the first time the stranger looked up and his eyes twinkled as he said, "Ah, but there soon will be."

The old woman replied, "How?"

The stranger licked his lips and said, "In my hands lies a magical secret ingredient. It has the power to create the best soup anyone has ever tasted."

The old woman said, "This I have to see."

The stranger sighed, "And I would gladly show you if I only had a large pot."

The old woman rubbed her head, feeling a light rumble of hunger in her stomach, and said, "A pot, eh? Wait here." She rushed to her cottage and scurried back clutching her largest pot.

The stranger sighed again and said, "I will need this pot filled with water so that my magic ingredient will make the most delicious soup you ever tasted."

Two strong men nearby hesitated for a moment and then grabbed four buckets, filled them at the well and emptied them into the pot.

The man held both hands over the pot of water. The villagers held their breath. The stranger pulled back his hands and said, "Ah, if only…."

The villagers cried, "Only what?"

The man said, "If only I had fire wood to heat this water. My secret ingredient will only work its magic in hot water."

The children of the village quickly scattered to collect dry wood for the fire. As soon as they returned a man stepped forward and lit a fire under the pot.

Once the water began to boil the man, once again, held both hands over the pot. There wasn't a sound to be heard in the village. The stranger then raised his head to the heavens and said, "But, but … something is missing."

The villagers looked to the heavens, then to the man and cried, "What … what could be missing?"

The man said, "If only I had a vegetable or two to add to my secret ingredient. Then the soup would taste heavenly."

Six women darted home and brought back handfuls of carrots, celery, onions and potatoes. The stranger watched as the vegetables were dumped into the pot. He again held his hands over the pot and again drew them back quickly. "I can't," is all he said.

The villagers exclaimed, "Why not?"

The man said, "There is one more thing that would make the soup so rich that the king himself, were he to taste it, would be envious."

The villagers cried, "Tell us! Tell us!"

He said sadly shaking his head, "I think…no, never mind."

No one spoke. A small voice asked, "Ham?"

The stranger replied, "Yes, ham."

No sooner was this said than an old woman hurried home and returned with a small ham. She dropped it into the steaming pot. As a savory aroma wafted through the air, the villagers shouted to the stranger, "Put your secret ingredient in *now*!"

The stranger smiled and said, "Gladly."

He then held his clenched fists over the bubbling pot and dramatically opened them. The villagers gasped as they watched a tiny pebble fall from the man's hands and plop into the soup.

They cried, "A pebble is the secret ingredient!"

The stranger replied, "But wait until you taste the soup."

After the villagers had filled their bowls and hungrily devoured all of the soup, they said to the stranger, "Yes, this was a soup fit for a king. And to think a pebble made it so delicious."

The stranger said, "But not just any pebble. Only a rare magical soup pebble. And because you have been so kind to me, I will leave this one with you so you will always be able to make such wonderful soup."

With that the stranger bid them farewell. As he began walking towards the next village the people of Luphen did not see that one of his pockets sagged from the weight of pebbles.

Whole-Language Activities for "The Secret Ingredient"

Before Reading Activities

Predicting vocabulary (p. 8)

This activity sheet is good for helping children predict words they think might be in the story. They will then read carefully to see if they were right.

Note: All of the words appear in the story except for forest.

During Reading Activities

Prepared reading

Many nonfluent readers never have an opportunity to read a selection well. Prepared reading gives such children an opportunity to practice assigned sections of a selection to a level of fluency prior to oral reading.

1. Divide the story into several logical parts and assign a student to each story part. These students are to:

   a. Practice reading the story section to themselves.

   b. Practice reading the story section aloud but very quietly.

   c. Select another student and practice reading the story section to them.

2. After the "story readers" are ready, have them read the story in correct sequence.

   Suggestion: Place a "Reader's Chair" in front of the group in which the reader may sit and read his or her section while the others listen.

After Reading Activities

Oral interpretation / Choral reading

1. Read the following verse orally with the students.

   It sounds really awful,
   I won't take a bite,
   You can't make me eat it,
   I'll put up a fight!

   Hey, what are you doing?
   What did you just add?
   Ham and potatoes!
   I'll have just a tad.

2. Now divide the room into three groups. One group will repeat "PEBBLE" on the first beat of each line, a second group will repeat "SOUP" on the second beat of each line, as the third reads the verse. It would look something like this:

It sounds really awful,
Pebble   Soup

I won't take a bite,
Pebble   Soup

You can't make me eat it,
Pebble   Soup

I'll put up a fight!
Pebble   Soup

Hey, what are you doing?
Pebble   Soup

What did you just add?
Pebble   Soup

Ham and potatoes!
Pebble   Soup

I'll have just a tad.
Pebble   Soup

3. Encourage your students to create their own choral readings. Divide them into groups and have each group develop and then demonstrate their own choral-reading version of the verse. They might want to use creative dramatic movements to enhance their readings.

Appropriate sequencing of dialogue

1. Copy each of the following on a different card.

"What are you doing?"

"I'm making my lunch."

"Lunch! Hunger must have made you daft, man. There's no food here."

"Ah, but there soon will be."

"How?"

"In my hands lies a magical secret ingredient. It has the power to create the best soup anyone has ever tasted."

"This I have to see."

"And I would gladly show you if I only had a large pot."

"A pot, eh. Wait here."

"I will need this pot filled with water so that my magic ingredient will make the most delicious soup you ever tasted."

"Ah, if only...."

"Only what?"

"If only I had a vegetable or two to add to my secret ingredient. Then the soup would taste heavenly."

"I can't."

"Why not?"

"There is one more thing that would make the soup so rich that the king himself, were he to taste it, would be envious."

"Tell us! Tell us!"

"I think...no, never mind."

"Ham?"

"Yes, ham."

"Put your secret ingredient in NOW!"

"Gladly."

"A pebble is the secret ingredient!"

"But wait until you taste the soup."

"Yes, this was soup fit for a king. And to think a pebble made it so delicious."

"But not just any pebble. Only a rare magical soup pebble. And because you have been so kind to me, I will leave this one with you so you will always be able to make such wonderful soup."

2. After you tell the following story to the children, pass out the cards so they are evenly distributed.

3. Now retell the story, only this time you will tell only the narrative part of the story. The students will read the dialogue on their cards when they think it is appropriate. For example:

YOU: The old woman said,

CHILD: This I have to see.

YOU: The man then looked at the woman and said,

CHILD: I do have one small problem, though.

Creative thinking / Story elaboration

1. Divide the students into committees, giving each committee a sheet of posterboard, felt-tipped pens, scissors, writing materials and assorted art materials.

2. Tell the committees that they are "advertising executives" and that each must come up with a scheme for marketing the soup from the folktale. They will need to create a name for it and then develop a promotional campaign to sell it to the rest of the class.

3. Each committee is to make a poster and write a brief commercial attempting to

sell the soup. They might even want to
include a give-away gift!

Suggestion: You may want to stimulate their
ideas by using the following example for a
commercial.

Stop…don't go out of your house without a
tummy full of Zippos Soup. It will make
you zip down the sidewalk. It will make
you zip through your homework. It will
make you zip through the school day.
Yes…zip, zip, zip, Zippos Soup for a real
Zip-a-Dee-Doo-Dah Day!

PREDICTING VOCABULARY

THE SECRET INGREDIENT

A long time ago a poor traveler happened upon a village. His clothes were ragged and torn and he carried no belongings. Now the villagers were poor themselves and what they did not need was a beggar coming to their homes. So when the villagers saw him, they quickly ran into their cottages and locked the doors.

The traveler thought to himself, "If I am going to get anything to eat in this village, I will have to use all my cunning."

This is the beginning of a folktale from Sweden called "The Secret Ingredient." Below is a list of words that could be in this story. Which ones do you think are "in" the story and which are the ones you think are "not." Write the words you think will be "in" the story in the pot.

1. lunch
2. magic
3. king
4. hungry
5. pebble
6. old woman
7. ham
8. boiling
9. forest
10. crazy

Now list the words you did not toss in the pot and tell why.

_____ _____

_____ _____

_____ _____

THE STONECUTTER

FOLKTALE FROM JAPAN

Once upon a time there was a stonecutter, named Sato, who lived next to a high mountain. Every day he would go to the mountain to work. He would cut out great chunks of stone to be used for gravestones or for houses. He was a poor but happy man.

Now in the mountain dwelt a great spirit. Some of the villagers talked about how this spirit had helped them in special ways. Sato had never seen the spirit but had no reason to doubt the villagers.

One day Sato carried a gravestone to the house of a rich man. He saw many beautiful things. On his way home he thought, "If only I had such a lovely house with such beautiful things. I would be the most powerful man in the village. How happy I would be."

A great voice thundered from the mountain and shook the ground on which Sato stood. "Your wish is my command. A beautiful home you shall have."

When Sato arrived home he was overwhelmed. Where once his shabby shack had been, there now rose a beautiful mansion. He hurried inside to find all the things he had ever wanted. "I shall be happy for the rest of my life," he said.

Weeks passes, then one day Sato was walking back from his work in the mountain. He was about to cross a street when a prince rode by in a golden carriage. Sato stood at the curb, frozen in mid-step, watching the beautiful carriage pass by. Once it was out of sight

he thought, "Oh, if only I were a rich prince. I would be the most powerful man in the country. How happy I would be."

The great voice once again thundered from the mountain. "Your wish is my command. A rich prince you shall be."

Sato now rode in a golden carriage with dozens of servants following him. But the day was very hot and no matter how much cool water he drank or how many servants fanned him, he was still hot. He looked up at the sun and shaking his fist said, "The sun is more powerful than I. If I were the sun then I would be the most powerful thing in the universe. And how happy I would be."

Again the great voice thundered from the mountain. "Your wish is my command. The sun you shall be."

And the sun he became. He now beamed with pride as he spread his rays over the earth, moon and far beyond. Then one day a large dark cloud covered his face. He became enraged. "How dare this cloud cover my face." He thought for a moment and then declared, "A cloud is more powerful than the sun. I wish to be a cloud and be the most powerful force in the world!"

The great voice thundered from the mountain. "Your wish is my command. A cloud you shall be."

And a cloud he was. He was now able to capture the sun's rays and not allow them to escape. So the days grew dark and cold. But this wasn't enough. He wanted to show that he had still more power, and so he rained down on the land for many days and nights. Whole villages were flooded and destroyed. Only the mountain of rock remained unmoved. The cloud was furious at the power of this mountain. He raged, "This mountain is more powerful than a cloud. I want to be a mountain of rock."

The great voice again thundered from the mountain. "Your wish is my command. A mountain of rock you shall be."

And the mountain he was. How he gloried in his power. At last he was the most powerful of things. He stood proudly looking down upon all those less powerful than him. Then one day he heard a strange noise. He looked down at his feet. There stood a small stonecutter chipping away at his base. He felt a trembling and a great block broke off and fell to the ground. He cried, "Is a mere stone-cutter mightier than a rock? Oh, if only I were a stonecutter."

The great voice thundered from the mountain. "Your wish is my command. A stonecutter once more you shall be."

And a stonecutter he was. From sun up to sun down he toiled as a stonecutter, never once longing to be someone or something else. He was happy at last and heard the great voice of the Mountain Spirit no longer.

Whole-Language Activities for "The Stonecutter"

Before Reading Activities

Paragraph building

1. Read the following to the students.

   The Stonecutter
   Once upon a time there was a stonecutter, named Sato, who lived next to a high stone mountain. Every day he would go to the mountain to work. He would cut out great chucks of stone to be used for gravestones or for houses. He was a poor but happy man.

2. Have every student write down a question they want answered from reading this story beginning. As the students read their questions, ask for volunteers to suggest possible answers.

3. Each student should now write down a sentence about the tall mountain. Ask the students to read their sentences aloud.

4. Now choose five or six students to go to the front of the classroom and stand next to one another, facing the class. Ask these students to read their sentences, going from left to right. Tell the class that these sentences can be made into a single paragraph. How would they change what the students have written to make one paragraph? They may want to change the order of the sentences and might even want to combine sentences.

5. Have them develop a "quality" paragraph from these five or six sentences by having the students reread their sentences after every couple of changes. This requires students to "listen" to what they are writing; a procedure they should always follow as they write but often times do not.

During Reading

Critical reading / Cause and effect (p.13)

This activity sheet will help students to read critically.

They are given certain events from the story and expected to write down the causes and predict their effects.

After Reading Activities

Pattern writing (p.14)

This activity sheet provides a simple writing pattern for students to follow.

Create an "I Want To Be..." bulletin board and attach the students finished papers for an informal self-evaluation.

Oral communication / Story extension

1. Using file folders, magazine pictures, scissors and glue make a supply of "Your Wish Is My Command" folders.

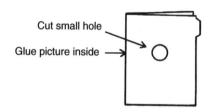

2. Pass these out to the students. They must not open the folder until they have tried to guess what the object is. They can do this by using clues they can see through the small hole. Tell the students that each folder is a picture of something the stonecutter wished for. Of course, the Mountain Spirit granted his wish by first saying "Your wish is my command."

3. Students should now take turns going to the front of the room and holding up the

folder for all to see. Next they will finish the following by guessing what is in the folder.

"Your wish is my command. You shall have…" (*their guess*)

4. Encourage the students to "become" the Mountain Spirit and not only tell what the object is but add other information about it as well.

For example: (a castle)

Your wish is my command. You shall have a castle in which to live. This castle will protect you from the rocks that regularly fall from my mountain. A high tower will be part of this castle. You may sit in the tower and watch your subjects go about their daily lives.

5. When the student is finished, she may open the folder in order to see if her guess was correct.

CRITICAL READING / CAUSE & EFFECT

THE STONECUTTER

When you reach an event in the story that is listed below, stop
reading and fill in the spaces, as in the example.

Event	Cause	Possible Effect
Sato wants a fine home.	He visited a rich man's home.	Spirit gives him one.
Sato wants to be a rich prince.		
The sun is angered by a cloud.		
Whole villages are flooded.		
The mountain wants to be a stonecutter.		

WRITING PATTERN

I want to be sick enough so Dad will bring me a present but not sick enough to have to take awful tasting medicine.

I want to be strong enough so the playground bully will leave me alone but not so strong that I break the merry-go-round by pushing too hard.

Now You Try It!

I want to be _____ enough so _____

but not _____ .

Choose one or more characters from "The Stonecutter." How would one of these characters write an "I Want To Be...?"

Example: The stonecutter wanted by be sick enough so he didn't have to go to the mountain and work but not sick enough to have to spend money for medicine.

Choose one: Stonecutter   Prince   Mountain Spirit

Write "I Want To Be..." about the character you chose:

_____
(character)

I want to be so_____ that _____

but not so_____ that _____ .

_____
(character)

I want to be so_____ that _____

but not so_____ that _____ .

THE CLEVEREST SON

AN ETHIOPIAN FOLKTALE

In a modest house on a small farm there once lived an old man with his three sons. Gondar and his three sons toiled from sun up to sun down and were often heard to say, "Ye reaps what ye sows." Well, it must have been true. Because of all of their hard work, they always had fine crops and never went hungry.

But one day, at the end of the growing season, Gondar grew sick and felt his end was near. He gathered his three sons into the house and said, "Sons, I am a sick old man and it is time for me to decide which of you will inherit the farm."

The first son quickly said, "But father, I am the oldest. It is only right that I inherit the farm."

The second son said loudly, "Nonsense. I have worked the hardest. I should inherit the farm."

"*You* work the hardest!" scoffed the first son. "Why I worked harder than the two of you combined!"

The third son, who had stood still with his head bowed, finally said quietly, "But father, you still have a long life ahead of you. Do not talk of dying."

A faint smile creased Gondar's face as he said, "It must be said, Jima."

All was quiet in the small house as the father continued. "Since you have indeed all worked very hard on our farm, I have decided upon a simple test to determine which of you

is the cleverest. Only that son will inherit the farm."

The three brothers looked at one another. Then the first son said, "Father, you know that I am the cleverest. Wasn't I the one who found the leak in the roof last year?"

The second son quickly said, "But I fixed the fence after the storm blew it over."

Jima continued to stand quietly with his head bowed.

"Yes," agreed the father, "you are all clever. But this test will determine which of you is the cleverest."

Pointing to the table, Gondar continued, "You see three coins on the table...one for each of you. Which ever of you buys something that will fill this room will inherit all I own."

The two older brothers each grabbed a coin and rushed out of the house.

"I can fill that puny little room," said the first son and dashed off toward the marketplace.

"What an easy task," laughed the second son and followed his brother toward the marketplace.

Jima stood staring at his father. Then he took the last coin from the table and slowly made his way to the marketplace deep in thought.

The first son chuckled at his cleverness as he went into a stall at the end of the marketplace. There he filled his wagon full of straw. "This is sure to fill up that puny room," he said smiling.

The second son thought a bit longer, then went to the other end of the market. There he bought sacks and sacks of feathers. "I am sure this is the cleverest anyone has ever been," he said grinning. "All of these feathers will surely fill up that small room."

Jima thought a very long time and then went into a small shop just off the market-place. He bought two small things and tucked them into his pocket.

That night the father called his sons into the house. "Now show me what your have bought that will fill up this room," he commanded.

The first son said proudly, "I bought straw that is sure to fill up this pun...ah, this room." He then hurried to bring in the wagon of straw. But it filled only one part of the room.

The second son said, "Ha! Straw! Now I bought something that is sure to fill up this room." He then hurried to bring in the sacks of feathers. But they filled only two corners of the room.

All eyes were now on Jima. He smiled faintly as he pulled the two small things out of his pocket, and soon filled the room.

"Yes," said the father, "you are indeed the cleverest and have filled my room when your brothers could not. You shall inherit my farm."

What had Jima bought that could both fit in his pocket and fill the room?

(*He bought a candle and a match and filled the room with light.*)

Whole-Language Activities for "The Cleverest Son"

Before Reading Activities

Critical thinking / Story pattern

Explain to the students that some folktales are really story riddles. For example, the following folktale is actually a riddle that has been told and retold for many generations in the United States.

Tell your students to listen carefully and see how many can figure out the correct answer. They are to write down their answers on paper, for later discussion.

Gone Fishing

Long ago two fathers and two sons went down to the river to fish. They fished all morning and by noon they each had caught one fish. As the two fathers and two sons walked back home, everyone was happy because each had a fish. When they got home they held up their fish for everyone to see. They held up three fish.

Two fathers and two sons. Only three fish and no fish were lost. How can this have happened?

(*Only three people went fishing. A boy, his father, and his grandfather: two sons and two fathers.*)

Story prediction / Discussion

1. Copy the following on the chalkboard.

   "The Cleverest Son"

   three brothers

   three coins

   inherit the farm

   one small room

2. Divide the students into groups. Each group is to focus on the title and story items on the chalkboard and decide what they think the folktale is about.

3. After each group has developed a simple story skeleton, have a group member share their ideas with the class.

4. Now read the folktale to find out if any of their predictions were correct.

During Reading Activities

Reading to verify predictions / Discussion

1. Have each group copy their story skeleton (from the Before Reading Activities) on a large sheet of paper. Attach these on a wall so all students may easily see them.

2. Now as you read the story, group leaders should place checks next to those predictions which are verified.

3. Discussion should follow the story. Questions are likely to arise as to the appropriateness of some of the verifications. Encourage students to read back through the folktale for confirmation.

After Reading Activities

Oral extension / Creative thinking

1. Tell students they will be meeting the father and his three sons from the folktale, "The Cleverest Son." They will be able to ask them questions in an interview situation. Therefore, they are each to write down four questions they would like to ask these characters.

   Suggestion: You might want to work through some group questions before the students develop their own. It is also advisable that students develop one question for each of the characters.

2. After giving the students adequate time in which to formulate their questions, place chairs in front of the group like this

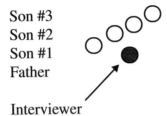

Son #3
Son #2
Son #1
Father

Interviewer

3. Now have the students take turns sitting in the interviewer's chair to ask their questions. Select volunteers to sit in the characters' chairs as indicated on the drawing. They are to answer the questions, feeling free to make up any of the information needed in their responses.

Writing dialogue pattern (p. 19)

This activity sheet provides an exercise in writing dialogue. Students are expected to fill in appropriate dialogue within the writing pattern given.

Suggestion: You might want to introduce the sheet and complete the first couple of sentences with suggestions from the students.

The completed dialogue sheets can be read aloud with different students reading the various characters' dialogue, in a Readers' Theater fashion. You may want to have a narrator in this case. Or you may choose to have them "act it out," much the same as actors reading their lines. In either case, allow the students time for a brief rehearsal.

WRITING DIALOGUE

THE CLEVEREST SON

Remember that the folktale ended with the father giving his youngest son his farm and house because he was the cleverest. He had filled the father's room with light from a candle. The other brothers had tried to fill the room, one with straw and the other with bags of feathers. But do you think this is all that was said? Do you really think that the two older brothers did not argue with the father's decision? Here is your chance to continue the "discussion!" You are to fill in the missing dialogue below. Make it serious or make it funny…but have *fun!*

"Yes," said the father, "you are indeed the cleverest and have filled my room when the others could not. You shall inherit my house and farm."

The oldest son stomped his foot and said, " _____
_____ !"

The father's face turned scarlet. He said, " _____
_____ ."

The youngest son added, "_____ "

The middle son, who had been standing very still, looked up and asked,
"_____ ?"

The father answered," _____
_____ ."

The oldest son then turned to leave the room. He said as he walked away,
"_____ ."

The father turned to him and said, "_____
_____ ."

The youngest son then ran to his oldest brother crying,
"_____ ."

The middle son sat down in the nearest chair and said, " _____
_____ ."

The father smiled and said, "_____ "

THE INVISIBLE WARRIOR

CANADIAN INDIAN FOLKTALE

It was a chilly spring evening many years ago. Moncton waited patiently on the shore of the great ocean as she did every evening. Soon her brother, Strong Wind, would arrive home from work.

Strong Wind was a great Indian warrior. He was known among his people as Strong Wind, the Invisible because of his strange powers to make himself unseen. This special power had made him a particular threat to his enemies, since he could go into their camps and learn of their plans without being noticed.

As Moncton peered out across the vast waters, she began to smile. She felt the breeze and knew Strong Wind would soon arrive. As always, they would go home together and eat the dinner she had prepared. This would be the last spring she would wait on the beach for Strong Wind. For this was to be the summer of Strong Wind's marriage.

All the maidens in the village wanted to be chosen to be the great Indian warrior's bride, but they would first have to pass the test. Above all else, Strong Wind desired truthfulness from his bride and so he and his sister had conceived a clever test that would judge the truthfulness of all who sought to win him.

The test was simple. The maiden would wait with Moncton for Strong Wind to come home from work in the twilight. Since the sister could always see Strong Wind, she would ask the maiden if she could see him the moment she did. If the maiden answered yes, the sister would ask further questions, like what was he wearing. In this way Strong Wind and the sister would always know if the maiden was not telling the truth.

Now there lived in the village a great chief who had three daughters. The youngest, Singing Bird, was very beautiful and gentle. The older sisters were jealous of her and dressed her in rags and cut off her long hair. Like the other maidens in the village the two older sisters wanted to marry Strong Wind. One evening they went down to the shore with Strong Wind's sister and waited. When Moncton saw him approaching, she asked the usual, "Do you see him?" And each one, lying, answered, "Yes." But when she asked further questions Strong Wind's sister knew they had lied and sent them both home.

Then one day the chief's youngest daughter, Singing Bird, went to seek Strong Wind. Her older sisters laughed at her and called her a fool. As she walked down to the beach all of the villagers laughed at her rags and ugly hair. Singing Bird kept her head down and silently continued walking to the beach.

"Welcome, Singing Bird," said Moncton kindly as the ragged girl arrived at the beach. "So you have come to take the test."

"Yes, Moncton," said Singing Bird quietly. "Please don't be mad."

"Mad!" exclaimed Moncton. "Why would I be mad?"

"Because I am so dirty and ugly. And surely Strong Wind would not want me for his bride."

Moncton had no time to answer Singing Bird for she saw Strong Wind coming home. She quickly asked, "Look, Moncton. Do you see him?"

Scanning the horizon Singing Bird answered, "No."

Moncton smiled at the girl and asked again, "Now do you see him?"

Singing Bird then smiled broadly and said, "Oh yes, and he is very wonderful."

Moncton then asked, "With what does he draw his sled?"

And Singing Bird answered, "With the rainbow."

Moncton then knew that because the girl had spoken the truth at first her brother had made himself visible to her. And she said, "Truly, you have seen him."

At once Singing Bird's rags were turned to fine clothes and her hair grew long and black like the raven's wing. "Come and take the wife's seat in the tent," said Moncton. And when she did, Strong Wind was beside her.

Soon the entire village celebrated the marriage of Strong Wind and Singing Bird. All, that is, except Singing Bird's two older sisters. As punishment for their cruelty to his wife, Strong Wind turned them each into an aspen tree and rooted them into the earth. And to this day the aspens' leaves tremble in fear at the approach of Strong Wind, no matter how softly he comes.

Whole-Language Activities for "The Invisible Warrior"

Before Reading Activities

Predicting story / Questioning

1. Divide your students into pairs or small groups. Tell them that they will be reading the Canadian Indian folktale, "The Invisible Warrior." But before they read it, you want them to find out how much of the story they can predict by finishing the following sentences:

An Indian warrior is…

Being invisible can be…

If you had to test someone's truthfulness you would…

"The Invisible Warrior" might be about…

Someone from each group must write down the group's ideas and be ready to read them to the class.

2. After each group has responded to the question beginnings, have the class vote on the predictions they think will come closest to the folktale.

3. Now read to find out if any are correct or which came nearest to the actual tale.

During Reading Activities

Critical thinking / Comparing tales (p.24)

1. Ask the students to tell you what they know about the folktale "Cinderella." List the information they give, such as, characters, settings and events.

2. Now pass out the activity sheet. The students should fill in as much of the sheet as they can from the class discussion and the information on the chalkboard.

3. Explain to the students that when they read "The Invisible Warrior," they should look for similarities and differences between the more familiar French version of "Cinderella" and this Canadian Indian version. They are to continue to fill in the activity sheet as they read the folktale.

After Reading Activities

Oral review of story sequence

1. Try this "Spin-a-Yarn" technique for a quick review of the story sequence. You will need to cut various lengths of yarn and then roll them, one by one, into a large ball of yarn prior to using this technique.

2. You should begin telling the folktale as you slowly unwind the ball of yarn. When you come to the end of your piece of yarn, pass the ball to a child who must then continue telling the story. She will do the same until she has unwound her piece of yarn, at which time she will hand it to the next storyteller. Continuing in this manner, the children will "spin-a-yarn."

Suggestion: You need to explain to the children that they may only unwind the yarn at the speed which they are telling the tale. In other words, they may not talk very slowly while they unwind the yarn as fast as they can! It is also advisable to tell the children that they may not unwind the yarn while they are saying things which do not further the story, such as, "uuuh," "and uh," etc.

Pattern writing (p.25)

This activity sheet provides a simple writing pattern for students to follow.

After the students have finished with this sheet, challenge them to use the same pattern to write sentences about Mother Goose characters. For example:

Humpty Dumpty saw *the King's Horses and the King's Men coming* and so *twirled around so fast on one foot* that *he fell off the wall.*

The poor old dog saw *the empty cupboard* and so *he barked and howled so loudly* that *Mother Hubbard rushed to the grocery to buy some milk bones*.

CRITICAL THINKING / COMPARING TALES

THE INVISIBLE WARRIOR

What are the similarities and differences between the familiar (French) version of Cinderella and the Canadian Indian version. Fill in as much of the information about the French version as you can from the class discussion and the information on the chalkboard.

Now read the Canadian Indian version, "The Invisible Warrior." Fill in the information as you read.

	Traditional (French) "Cinderella"	Canadian Indian "The Invisible Warrior"
Characters	Cinderella: youngest/stepsister	Singing Bird: youngest sister
Settings		
"Magical Powers"		

Complete these sentences:

In both folktales <u>the older sisters were cruel to their younger sister</u> and/but <u>they were punished</u>.

In both folktales_____

_____and/but _____ .

In both folktales_____

_____and/but _____ .

In both folktales_____

_____and/but _____ .

PATTERN WRITING

THE INVISIBLE WARRIOR

Complete the following lists by adding describing words under each of the characters:

Strong Wind	Great Chief	Strong Wind's Sister	Singing Bird	Older Sisters
powerful	proud	faithful	beautiful	cruel

Strong Wind saw the cruelty of Singing Bird's sisters and so he turned them into aspens that always trembled with fear at his presence.

The older sisters saw Singing Bird's beauty and so dressed her in rags that made her look ugly.

Now you try this writing pattern! Use your describing words to help.

_____ saw _____ and so

_____ that _____.

_____ saw _____ and so

_____ that _____.

THREE MAGIC ORANGES

FOLKTALE FROM COSTA RICA

It was nearing the end of the summer season when King Atenas called for his son. As Prince Cinco entered his father's room, the king said, "Son, I've become greatly concerned for you."

"Father, why would you be concerned? Have I done something?" asked Prince Cinco.

"No, my son. Indeed, it is what you have not done which concerns me," said his father.

"I don't understand?" said the prince looking quite puzzled.

"It's the matter of a wife," said King Atenas. "I am getting old and I don't want to die without seeing you with a wife."

"Oh father, there is plenty of time for that," laughed the prince.

"*No more time*!" stormed the king. "You will find a wife *now*!"

"But father…" stammered Prince Cinco.

"*No!!!*" interrupted his father. "I said now and I mean *now*! You will, this day, go into the country and find a wife. And do not return until you have done so."

"But…"

"Be gone with you this instant. And don't return without a wife!" King Atenas whirled around and left the prince standing alone in the room.

The young prince did as his father had ordered. He saddled his favorite horse and rode off into the countryside in search of a bride. At the edge of a great forest he saw a handsome orange tree with three large golden oranges. He rode over to the tree and plucked them. After packing them in his saddle bag, he continued on his journey, thinking, "A wife. That is what I must find. Can't go back without one. Must find one."

The sun was hot and the road was dusty and he grew very thirsty, but there wasn't a spring or stream in sight. Being the end of the summer season, it had not rained for a long time. He went on, on, and on and still no water. Then he remembered the juicy oranges in his saddle bag. Quickly he took one out and cut it in two with his knife. As he did this a puff of orange smoke exploded in his face. When it cleared, a beautiful maiden stood before him.

"Please oh please, I beg of you,
A drink of water will only do."

The prince was stunned but he managed to say, "I cannot give what I do not have." There came another burst of orange smoke and when it cleared the beautiful maiden had vanished. Prince Cinco stared as the last trace of orange smoke disappeared and thought, "two more oranges in the saddle bag." He decided not to open another one so readily. He ate the juicy orange and continued on his way. But the road seemed even hotter and dustier than before. And he became thirstier than he had ever been in his life. So he took another orange from his pocket and sliced it open.

Again, a puff of orange smoke exploded in his face. When it cleared another maiden, more beautiful than the first, stood before him.

"Please oh please, I beg of you,
A drink of water will only do."

Prince Cinco was struck by her intense beauty but could only answer, "I cannot give what I do not have." Another orange cloud exploded and the maiden was gone. The prince stood in wonder as he slowly ate the second juicy orange.

"I shall not cut open the last orange until I am near water," he promised to himself and continued on his way.

It seemed to be getting hotter and dustier along the trail. He had never known such thirst. He felt parched as he rode slowly under the broiling sun. It was then he heard the sound of bubbling spring water. He ran to the mossy bank and took a long drink. Then taking out the last orange, he hesitated for only a moment before cutting it open.

Once again, an explosion of orange smoke was followed by a beautiful maiden, this one was the most beautiful maiden of all.

"Please oh please, I beg of you,
A drink of water will only do."

Not waiting a moment the prince scooped up some water in the hollow of his hand and raised it to her lips.

"You've broken the evil spell," exclaimed the maiden. "Finally I am free."

"Evil spell?" questioned the prince.

"Yes, long ago a wicked witch cast her spell and turned me into the orange you plucked from the tree. I have waited a long time for a prince to come by and break the evil spell."

Prince Cinco fell in love with the beautiful maiden immediately and said, "Please come back to the palace with me. I've someone who is waiting to meet you."

As Prince Cinco helped the maiden onto the horse he added, "My father, King Atenas, will be so happy."

By the time the two reached the palace they were very much in love. The kingdom was soon ringing with wedding bells and, yes, they lived happily ever after. Oh yes, there is now growing on the palace grounds a handsome orange tree with two large golden oranges.

Whole-Language Activities for "Three Magic Oranges"

Before Reading Activities

Creative thinking / Story prediction

1. Copy the following on the chalkboard.

How would you look if:

- you were a king who was ordering his son to find a wife.

- you came across a handsome orange tree bearing three large golden oranges.

- you were on a long journey on horseback and the trail was very hot and dusty.

- you cut open an orange and a beautiful maiden appeared before you.

- you were dying of thirst and you suddenly found a bubbling spring.

- your life had been saved by a prince.

- you fell completely in love with a beautiful maiden/prince.

2. Now explain to the students that they will each have a turn standing in front of the group and demonstrating how they would look if they were in one of the situations described on the chalkboard. The other students will try to guess which one they are demonstrating.

   Suggestion: You might want to begin with the students pantomiming the situations and having them concentrate only upon facial and body expression. Later, they might want to add dialogue.

Attentive listening / Chalk talk

1. Tell the students the following story prior to reading "Three Magic Oranges."

2. Simply draw the lines shown below in the story as you tell it.

Long ago lived a young prince. He loved playing in the palace yard with his friends. The palace yard circled the palace...

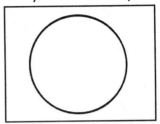

...and offered ample room to play the many games he and friends loved. But today as he left the palace to go looking for his friends he noticed something new in the palace grounds. It was a well.

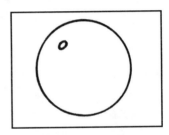

"That well wasn't here yesterday," Prince Cinco said to himself. "How could the peasants have dug that well during the night? Impossible? But then..."

Just then he heard a voice. "Come over here, Princy." Prince Cinco looked around but didn't see anyone. "Over here, the well, Princy. And get a move on. I don't have all day, you know."

The prince walked over to the well wondering if he was dreaming. "Stick your head in, Princy."

"See here," said the prince. "No one calls me Princy."

"My my my...a bit touchy aren't we. But never mind. Princy, do I have a deal for you."

"What?"

"Are you hard of hearing, Princy? I said I have a great deal for you. Now listen up! You must find two rocks that look like lizards.

28

When you find them throw them in the well. If you don't take all day, I'll grant you a wish. Now hop to!"

Prince Cinco didn't waste any time. He began digging small holes all over the palace grounds...

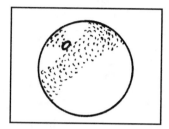

...until he finally found a rock that looked like a lizard. He hurried back and tossed it in the well. He heard a loud thud and then a big splash of water came out of the well.

"For goodness sake, would you please give a person a warning next time. You hit me square on my head! Now hurry up and find the second rock."

Prince Cinco rushed to the other side of the palace grounds and began digging. He dug up most of the ground when at last he found another lizard shaped rock.

He was so excited that he forgot to give a warning and tossed it in the well. "Ooofff!" came a loud groan from the bottom of the well. And then another splash of water. But

this time the splash made a direct landing on the prince. A chuckle came from deep in the well. "Okay, Princy. What is your wish... and make it snappy!"

The prince thought for a long time and then he made his wish. What do you think it was?

(A Magic Orange!)

During Reading Activities

Oral communication / Oral reading

A particularly useful oral reading technique for nonfluent readers is "Double Does It." This technique requires the pairing of students.

In each pair one student reads a paragraph and then the second student reads the same paragraph plus the next paragraph. Now it is back to the first student to reread the second paragraph and continue reading the third.

This "back-and-forth technique continues throughout the story. This allows each child to hear material read immediately prior to their own oral reading.

Alternative: You might pair fluent readers with nonfluent readers, having the fluent reader read each paragraph first. This enables the nonfluent reader to hear a good model just preceding their own reading.

After Reading Activities

Attentive listening

1. Explain to the students that you will reread the end of the folktale and they

should carefully listen. Begin reading with this paragraph:

It seemed to be getting hotter and dustier along the trail. He had never known such thirst. He felt parched as he rode slowly under the broiling sun. It was then he heard…

2. Now tell the students you will once again read this ending but this time you are going to make changes in the story. They are to attempt to note these changes. They may want to write them down as you read the following: *(the underlined words/phrases are the changes from the original)*

It seemed to be getting hotter and dustier along the trail. He had never known such thirst. His <u>mouth felt dry</u> as he rode slowly under the broiling sun. It was then he heard the sound of <u>water running in a river.</u> He ran to the mossy bank and took a long drink. Then taking out the last orange, he hesitated for only a moment before cutting it open.

Once again, an explosion of orange smoke was followed by a beautiful maiden this one was the most beautiful of all.

"Please oh please, I beg of you,
A drink of water will only do.
<u>The prince hesitated briefly then</u> scooped up some water in the hollow of his hand and raised it to her lips.

"You've broken the evil spell," exclaimed the maiden. "Finally I am free."

"Evil spell?" questioned the prince.

"Yes, long ago a wicked <u>demon</u> cast a spell and turned me into the orange you plucked from the tree. I have waited a long time for a prince to come by and break the evil spell."

Prince Cinco fell in love with the beautiful maiden immediately and said, "There is someone I want you to meet who is back at my palace. Please <u>let me help you onto my horse</u> so I might take you there."

As Prince Cinco helped the maiden onto the horse he added, "My father, King Atenas, will be so happy."

By the time the two reached the palace they were very much in love. The Kingdom was soon ringing with wedding bells and, yes, they lived happily ever after. Oh yes, there is now growing on the palace grounds a handsome orange tree with <u>three</u> large golden oranges.

Inductive reasoning / Discussion skills

1. Read the following to the students:

By the time the two reached the palace they were very much in love. The Kingdom was soon ringing with wedding bells and, yes, they lived happily ever after.

2. Tell the students that this was not true. Actually, they were happy for a very brief period because something terrible happened to them. The class will be able to find out what happened to them by using the clues on the cards you've prepared. If they organize the clues correctly, they will know the "real" story of Prince Cinco and his bride.

3. The students should sit in a circle facing one another. Now distribute the cards evenly to each student. They can unravel the real story by sharing their clues *but*…this must be done orally. The cards may *not* be passed around the group.

4. Copy each of the following clues on a different index card and distribute them to the students. Students may have more than one card, just so all cards are passed out. Tell the students they must be able to complete the "rest of the story" in the proper story sequence. *(The clues are in the correct order below.)*

Soon after the wedding King Atenas dies.

Prince Cinco and his wife become King and Queen of the land.

Wicked witch hears news of happy King and Queen.

Witch disguises self as a poor woman.

A poor woman selling fruit and pins starts out for palace.

Queen calls woman into the palace.

Queen likes the pearl pin.

Witch thrusts the pearl pin into the Queen's head.

Queen is turned into a white dove.

A white dove flies into the forest.

While hunting the King sees a white dove.

King captures white dove to take back to Queen.

King returns to palace with white dove.

Queen has disappeared from the palace.

King grieves for his missing Queen.

While petting white dove the King feels a pin in its head.

Carefully the King removes the pearl pin.

The white dove vanishes.

The Queen appears before the King.

The Queen tells King what the witch had done.

King orders men to find witch.

Witch brought back to palace and locked in dungeon.

Now the King and Queen live happily ever after!

THE DISAPPEARING DONKEY

ARABIAN FOLKTALE

One day an old farmer walked along a dusty road to the town, leading his donkey by a rope. The farmer was thinking of what he would buy at the market, so he did not notice two thieves hiding under a bush beside the road.

"Jidda," whispered the one thief to the other. "I am going to steal that donkey."

Yaubu looked at his friend and asked, "In broad daylight?"

"Yes. Just do as I tell you." They put their heads together. Then they got up and went after the farmer and the donkey. They walked very softly along the dusty road and the farmer didn't hear them. Jidda took the rope off the donkey's neck and put it around his own neck. And Yaubu led the donkey away from the road.

After a while the farmer looked back at his donkey, but it was gone. Instead a man was following with a rope around his neck. The farmer stopped dead in his tracks. He could hardly believe his eyes.

"Who...who...are you?" stammered the farmer.

"I know you're surprised," said Jidda smiling. "I've been your donkey for a long time. But I never was really a donkey. Because of the many terrible things I'd done, I was changed into a donkey. I've worked hard for you to show how sorry I was for doing wrong. Your many beatings have paid for all of my wrongdoing and now I've been changed back into a man again."

The farmer was astounded by the story, but he saw the man where his donkey had been. He had to believe what the man told him.

"I guess I must let you go," said the farmer. "I don't know what I shall do without a donkey. I have to buy some things at the market and so I expect that I'll have to carry them home on my back."

"I'm sorry for you," said Jidda. "You have all of my good wishes. I hope that you'll soon get another donkey but now I must say 'goodbye' to you."

Jidda then turned and walked away. He went back along the road where he found Yaubu and the donkey hiding in the bushes. The two thieves laughed and laughed at the joke they had played upon the farmer. Later that day they sold the donkey in the nearest town. Looking at their money Yaubu said, "This has been a good day's work."

A few days later the farmer went to town to buy a new donkey. While looking at the animals for sale, he suddenly came across one that looked strangely familiar.

"It is...No! Can it be...?" stammered the farmer. Carefully studying the donkey, he recognized his own brand mark on its back.

"Good heavens!" shouted the farmer. "You scoundrel! Just a few days as a human being and you're at it again. When will you give up your bad ways? No wonder you were changed back into a donkey."

The donkey lifted his head and brayed.

"That does it!" the farmer exclaimed. "I'll show you! This time I *won't* buy you. I'll leave the likes of you to another master."

Quite pleased with himself, the farmer walked away.

Whole-Language Activities for "The Disappearing Donkey"

Before Reading Activities

Vocabulary and story prediction (p. 35)

Before passing out this activity sheet, read the first part of the folktale to the students. Read through "And Yaubu led the donkey away from the road."

During Reading Activities

Story prediction / Critical thinking / Oral communication

1. Choose four students to preread the story. Assign each of these students to be one of the characters. (Old Farmer, Jidda, Yaubu, and the Donkey)

2. Now tell the students that they are to imagine themselves on a panel of the popular television show called "Are You Telling the Truth?" On today's program they will have four guests. Introduce the four "characters" and explain they are from a folktale titled "The Disappearing Donkey."

3. The "panel" will have the opportunity to ask these four guests each five questions about their roles in the story. The guests may answer truthfully or not.

4. After the twenty questions have been answered, divide the students into groups. Each group is to decide what they think the story is going to be about, citing as many details as possible. Each group should report back their findings to the whole class.

5. Now read the story.

After Reading Activities

Story elaboration / Character interpretation

1. Copy the following on the chalkboard or transparency.

   How would you look if:

   • you were an old farmer leading a donkey down a hot dusty road.

   • you had just tricked an old farmer out of a donkey.

   • you turned to look at your donkey but instead there is a man in the harness.

   • an old farmer finds his missing donkey.

   • an old farmer thinks he has the better of his donkey.

   (take student suggestions)

2. Now explain to the students that they will each have a turn standing in front of the group, demonstrating how they would look if they were in one of the situations described on the chalkboard. The other students will try to guess which one they are demonstrating.

   Suggestion: You might want to begin with the students pantomiming the situations and having them concentrate only upon facial and body expression. Later, they might want to add dialogue.

Story elaboration / Oral reading (p. 36)

This activity sheet will provide students with a complete story review by asking them to "update" the story: that is, place the story in contemporary times.

Students will enjoy sharing their updated versions. Encourage them to practice reading their stories to a partner prior to reading them to the entire class.

VOCABULARY & STORY PREDICTION

THE DISAPPEARING DONKEY

What words do you think you may find in this story?
Write them in the proper lists below.

"things	"actions"	"places"	"emotions"
rope	running	town	surprised

Below is a cartoon strip. You are to tell what you think will happen
in the story by drawing in the cartoons. You *must* write what the
characters are saying in the cartoon bubbles, as shown in the first
cartoon frame. Use some of the words listed above.

STORY ELABORATION / ORAL READING

"The Disappearing Donkey" took place a long time ago in Arabia. How might it be told if it took place today in your neighborhood?

First change the characters and situation:

Long Time Ago	Today
old farmer	school principal
Jidda, thief	Dork, playground bully
Yaubu, thief	Sleze, Dork's sidekick
donkey	brief case

Now for the beginning of an "updated" version:

It was morning as Mr. Peacock walked across the playground on his way to work. He was carrying his brief case, as usual. Dork and Sleze were hiding in the bushes next to the sidewalk. As Mr. Peacock passed by, Sleze stuck out his foot and tripped him. After he picked himself up, he looked for his brief case. But instead of seeing his briefcase, he saw Dork on the ground.

Now you try!

Long Time Ago	Today
old farmer	_____
Jidda, thief	_____
Yaubu, thief	_____
donkey	_____
donkey is stolen	_____

Updated Version:

_____

_____

_____

_____

_____

GUILTY OR NOT GUILTY

JEWISH FOLKTALE

The people of Seville were all talking about the robbery that had just taken place. Imagine, a robbery taking place in the home of the Grand Judge! The Grand Judge was furious and wanted someone to pay for this crime. Unfortunately for the Rabbi, the Grand Judge did not much care if the person was guilty or not guilty, as long as someone was brought to trial.

Now the Grand Judge hated the Rabbi and was only too glad to see him brought to his courtroom. Despite all of his efforts, though, the Grand Judge could not prove the Rabbi was the thief.

Looking out upon the people in the court room the Grand Judge said, "We will leave the judgment of the matter to God. Let there be a drawing of lots. I shall deposit two pieces of paper in a box. On one I shall write the word "guilty." There shall be no writing on the other paper. If the Rabbi draws the first paper, it will be a sign from Heaven that he is guilty and will go to prison. If he draws the second, God will have given proof of his innocence and he shall go free."

Now the Grand Judge was a very sly fellow. He figured he could write guilty on both pieces of paper and no one would ever know. The Rabbi suspected he was going to do just this. Therefore, when he put his hand into the box and drew forth a piece of paper he quickly put it into his mouth and swallowed it.

The Grand Judge raged, "What is the meaning of this! How will we ever know what was on the piece of paper?"

The Rabbi replied, "Very simple. You have only to look at the paper in the box."

So they took out the paper still in the box.

"There!" cried the Rabbi. "This paper says guilty. Therefore the one I swallowed must have been blank. I am not guilty!"

And the Grand Judge had to let him go free.

Whole-Language Activities for "Guilty or Not Guilty"

Before Reading Activities

Brainstorming story possibilities (p. 41)

This activity sheet is designed to help students work through a simple discussion of the possible elements of the story they are to read.

Have the students complete the sheet prior to the discussion. Encourage them to share and compare their ideas during the brainstorming session.

During Reading Activities

Reader's theater / Problem solving

1. Use the following version of "Guilty or Not Guilty" for a reader's theater activity. Simply select volunteers for each of the characters and read through the script.

2. You will notice at one point in the script that students are to stop reading and discuss the possible climax of the story.

3. At the end of the story have the students attempt to decide how the Rabbi knew which piece of paper to swallow.

Guilty or Not Guilty — A Reader's Theater

Characters: Grand Judge, Rabbi, Lawyer for the Prosecution, Lawyer for the Defense, Chief of Police, Court Official, Narrator.

Official: All rise. The court of Seville is now in session.

Judge: Rabbi, you stand accused of breaking into private property and stealing 50 gold pieces. How do you plead?

Rabbi: Not guilty.

Judge: Did you say, "Not guilty?"

Rabbi: Yes, not guilty.

Judge: Do you mean to stand there and say that you did not break into my house last night and steal 50 gold pieces?

Rabbi: Yes, your honor. I did not break into your house last night and steal 50 gold pieces.

Judge: Not guilty indeed. We shall see about that! Prosecutor, call your first witness.

Prosecutor: I call the Chief of Police to the stand. Tell me, Chief, did you arrest the Rabbi?

Chief: Yes, I did.

Prosecutor: Why?

Chief: Well, the Judge called me to his house late last night and told me that someone had broken in and had stolen 50 gold pieces. When I asked the Judge who might have done such a thing, he told me that he was positive that the Rabbi had done it. So I arrested the Rabbi.

Prosecutor: Why were you so sure though that the Rabbi might have stolen the gold pieces?

Chief: When I got the Rabbi's house I found the Rabbi unlocking his front door. He was holding a bag that contained 50 gold pieces.

Prosecutor: Thank you.

Judge: Defense, do you have any questions?

Defense: No questions.

Judge: Prosecutor, call your next witness.

Prosecutor: I call to the stand, the Rabbi. When the Chief arrested you, were you holding a bag that contained 50 gold pieces?

Rabbi: Yes.

Prosecutor: Did those 50 gold pieces belong to you?

Rabbi: No.

Prosecutor: Whose gold pieces were they?

Rabbi: They belonged to the judge.

Prosecutor: No further questions.

Judge: You see, I knew you were guilty Rabbi. Just to be fair, I will let the Defense ask you some questions.

Defense: Rabbi, do you always tell the truth?

Rabbi: Yes.

Defense: Rabbi, when the Chief arrested you, why were you standing outside your front door?

Rabbi: I was locking it.

Defense: You were locking it. Why?

Rabbi: I was going to see the Judge.

Defense: Why were you going to see the Judge?

Rabbi: To return his 50 gold pieces to him.

Defense: Why would you do that?

Rabbi: Earlier that evening, after I had just fallen asleep, the Judge came to see me. Still sleepy, I asked him to come in. We talked for a while and then he left. After he had gone, I noticed that he had left a bag on my table. When I opened it, I discovered 50 gold pieces. I thought that such an important man as the Judge should not leave his gold pieces lying about. So I got dressed and was preparing to take the gold back to the Judge when the Chief arrested me.

Defense: So you did not steal the gold?

Rabbi: No.

Defense: And you were on your way to the Judge's house to return the gold to him?

Rabbi: Yes.

Defense: So you did not break into the Judge's house?

Rabbi: Certainly not. I was in bed asleep.

Defense: No further questions.

Judge: I will leave this up to the jury to decide. Jury you must decide whether this Rabbi is guilty or not guilty.

(At this point allow students to voice opinions as to the Rabbi's guilt or innocence.)

Judge: The jury is taking too much time. I will decide this case myself. To show that I am not partial, I will leave the judgment to God. Let there be a drawing of lots. I shall deposit two pieces of paper in a box. On one I shall write the word "guilty." There shall be no writing on the other paper. If the Rabbi draws the first paper, it will be a sign from Heaven that he is guilty and will go to prison. If he draws the second, God will have given proof of his innocence and he shall go free.

Narrator: The Rabbi reached into the box and drew out a piece of paper. Quickly he popped the paper into his mouth and swallowed it.

Judge: What is the meaning of this? Why did you swallow that paper? How will we ever know what was written on it?

Rabbi: Very simple. You have only to look at the paper in the box.

Judge: Very well, we shall look.

Rabbi: There! This paper from the box says guilty. Therefore the one I swallowed must have been blank. I am not guilty!

Judge: Case dismissed. You are free to go.

(How did the Rabbi know which piece of paper to swallow?

Answer: *The Grand Judge had always hated the Rabbi. The Judge had deliberately left his 50 gold pieces on the Rabbi's table so that it might appear as if the Rabbi had stolen the gold. Also, the Judge was a sly fellow. When he decided to draw lots, he wrote the word "guilty" on both pieces of paper, figuring that when the Rabbi drew out a piece of paper it would say "guilty." The Rabbi thought the Judge would try to trick him in this way, so he swallowed the piece of paper, knowing that both of them said "guilty."*

After Reading Activities

Oral extensions

1. Explain to the students they are now going to play a game called "Keep Talking." You will pass out a card to each student. This card contains a phrase which was in the folktale.

2. The students will take turns standing in front of the group and talking about something. During this talk they must include the phrase on their card. The rest of the students will attempt to guess the phrase when the student finishes. Be sure to allow ample planning time for this activity.

   Phrases to place on cards:

about the robbery	drawing of lots
was furious	write the word
pay for this crime	draws the second
have given proof	go to prison
he is guilty	into the box
pieces of paper	took out the paper
let him go	must have been blank
will be a sign	upon the people
brought to trial	could not prove

Critical thinking

1. After having read both versions of "Guilty or Not Guilty," copy the following on the chalkboard:

   "Similarities"   "Differences"

2. Divide the students into small groups and have them discuss the similarities and differences between the two versions of the folktale.

   Suggestion: You may want to begin this activity as a whole class so each group will understand what it is they are expected to do.

3. Now using the students' suggestions, make a class list of those things that are the same in each story and a list of those things that are different.

BRAINSTORMING STORY POSSIBILITIES

GUILTY OR NOT GUILTY

This story takes place a very long time ago in Spain. It is about a Rabbi accused of robbing the Grand Judge.

What do you think the Rabbi is accused of stealing?

_____

Why do you think the Rabbi is accused of the theft?

_____

Make a drawing showing where you think most of the action takes place in this story.

```
┌─────────────────────────────────────────────┐
│                                               │
│                                               │
│                                               │
│                                               │
│                                               │
│                                               │
│                                               │
└─────────────────────────────────────────────┘
```

The Rabbi is taken to a Judge. Do you think he will be found guilty or not guilty?_____

This is how the Rabbi looks at the end of the story.

This is how the Grand Judge looks at the end of the story.

CRASH IS COMING

FOLKTALE FROM RUSSIA

Characters: Narrator, Two Squirrels, Rabbit, Fox, Deer, Eagle.

Narrator: One day two squirrels were playing tag and were leaping from tree to tree. They were having so much fun that they didn't notice a tree full of dead branches just ahead of them. When both squirrels jumped onto a limb that was rotten inside, the limb made a great snap! Then it fell to the ground with a mighty crash! Luckily, the squirrels were not hurt when the limb snapped. They jumped to safety.

First Squirrel: Oh! Did you hear that terrible noise?

Second Squirrel: Oh! Yes, I heard it. It was terrible. But who made that noise?

First Squirrel: I don't know. But whoever made it must be very strong. We should flee from here. Imagine if that noisemaker comes back!

Narrator: And so, the two squirrels scampered through the forest. They had not run far when they met Rabbit.

Rabbit: Why are you running?

First Squirrel: Because Crash is coming! We just heard him!

Fox: Crash? Who is Crash?

Second Squirrel: We don't know. But he can tear branches from trees and hurl them to the ground.

Rabbit: Yes, and he can also pull entire trees out of the ground! You must run for your life!

Narrator: And so, Fox, Rabbit and the two squirrels bolted through the forest. They had not run far when they met Deer, who was grazing on some sweet grass.

Deer: Why are you running?

First Squirrel: Because Crash is coming! We just heard him!

Deer: Who is Crash?

Second Squirrel: We don't know. But he can tear branches from trees and hurl them to the ground.

Rabbit: Yes, and he can also pull entire trees out of the ground with just one hand!

Fox: Yes, and he can also knock down a whole forest of trees with just one stomp of his foot! You must run for your life!

Narrator: And so, Deer, Fox, Rabbit, and the two squirrels raced through the forest in search of safety. They hadn't run very far when they met Eagle.

Eagle: Why are all of you running?

First Squirrel: Because Crash is coming! We just heard him!

Eagle: Who is Crash?

Second Squirrel: We don't know. But he can tear branches from trees and hurl them to the ground.

Rabbit: Yes, and he can also pull entire trees out of the ground with just one hand!

Fox: Yes, and he can also knock down a whole forest of trees with just one stomp of his foot! You must run for your life!

Deer: Yes, and he can knock down mountains just by sneezing at them! You must run for your life!

Eagle: Tell me, Deer, did you see Crash sneeze away a mountain?

Deer: No. Fox told me about Crash.

Eagle: Tell me, Fox, did you see Crash stomp down an entire forest?

Fox: No. Rabbit told me about Crash.

Eagle: Tell me, Rabbit, did you see Crash pull entire trees out of the ground?

Rabbit: No. The squirrels told me about Crash.

Eagle: Tell me, Squirrels, did you see Crash tear branches from trees and hurl them to the ground?

Squirrels: Yes, we did!

Eagle: You must show me where you saw Crash do this.

Narrator: And so, the two squirrels led Eagle back through the forest to the tree where they first heard the terrible sound of Crash. Deer, Fox, and Rabbit followed along.

First Squirrel: This is the place where we first heard Crash.

Second Squirrel: Yes, this is the tree where Crash tore the branch and hurled it to the ground.

First Squirrel: Look. Here is the branch that he threw to the ground this morning.

Eagle: Do you see? Crash is not someone terrifying. Crash is just the sound a dead branch makes when it fall to the ground. What is so terrifying about that? Why should that sound make you almost run your legs off?

Deer: Well, Fox told me.

Fox: Well, Rabbit told me.

Rabbit: Well, the squirrels told me.

First Squirrel: Well, it's all your fault. You wanted to play tag.

Second Squirrel: No, it's not my fault. You picked this tree to play in.

Narrator: At that moment, Eagle flew up into the air. He landed on one of the dead branches of the tree that the squirrels had been playing in earlier. Eagle hadn't been sitting on the dead branch very long when it suddenly went snap! The dead branch then fell to the ground with a mighty *crash!* The Eagle then landed beside the other animals. The other animals stopped arguing. They quietly went their own ways and never spoke of Crash again.

Whole-Language Activities for "Crash Is Coming"

Before Reading Activities

Language flexibility (p. 46)

This activity sheet is designed to acquaint students with figurative language. Students will discover what onomatopoeia is (the use of words in which their pronunciations suggest their meaning) by using the thinking skills of fluency and flexibility.

Students should think of as many different things as possible that can produce the sounds listed on the activity page. Divergent answers can be encouraged as long as the student can explain his/her reasoning. This activity will allow students to explore a secondary sense (sound) by seeing how closely tied to sound language is.

Sound & sense (p. 47)

1. After students have answered each question on the activity page, they should then think of a reason why they made the choice they did. Questions to consider if, for example, a student were to write that "crash is louder than plop."

   Why is crash louder?

   What things crash? What things plop?

   Can a plop ever be louder than a crash? Why? Why not?

2. Other questions to consider after the students have completed the activity page:

   Which sound is the most peaceful? the most annoying? the scariest? the funniest? the most hopeful? the saddest? the happiest? the absolute loudest?

   In the story, "Crash Is Coming," the animals of the forest are running from a tremendous sound. What do you think that sound might be? Why would the animals be running?

Make some predictions as to why the animals are running. Make some predictions as to what or who made the sound "crash."

During Reading Activities

Sound & action story

1. Think of a sound and/or a movement that the entire class can make after each animal tells the terrible things that Crash can do. For example, when the Second Squirrel tells Rabbit, "Crash can tear branches from trees and hurl them to the ground," the entire class might clap their hands and say, "Crash!"

2. Repeat this when Squirrel tells the same thing to Fox and, after Rabbit says, "Crash can pull entire trees out of the ground!" the class might then tear sheets of paper and say, "Rrrrrip!"

3. Repeat this when Squirrel and Rabbit tell the same thing to Deer, and after Fox says, "Crash can also knock down a whole forest of trees with just one stomp!" the class might then stomp their feet and say "Tim-ber!"

4. Repeat this when Squirrel, Rabbit, and Fox tell the same thing to Eagle, and when Deer says, "Crash can knock down mountains just by sneezing at them!" the class might cup their hands over their mouths and yell, "Ah-choo!"

5. The sequence would be as follows:

   After Squirrel's line each time: Clap hands twice and say, "Crash!"

   After Rabbit's line each time: Tear sheet of paper and say, "Rrrrrip!"

   After Fox's line each time: Stomp feet twice and say, "Tim-ber!"

After Deer's line each time: Cup hands over mouth and yell, "Ah-choo!"

After Reading Activities

Language application *(p. 48)*

1. Read the four Mother Goose rhymes aloud that are on the activity page.

2. Students should choose the word(s) that best describe(s) the sound that they infer from hearing the rhyme.

3. Students should then explain their reasons for choosing the word they did.

   Suggestion: Ask students to investigate other Mother Goose rhymes or other poems. As they read they should pick onomatopoeic words that apply.

Word Jazz *(p. 49)*

1. Students can develop new language patterns through energized choral reading. The Word Jazz is a rhythmic construction of language which emphasizes both rhyme and onomatopoeia.

2. Divide the class into two groups: A and B. Assign solo parts to eight different students.

3. Now practice reading Word Jazz, on the activity sheet, a number of times, each time working for greater rhythm, smoothness and energy.

   Suggestion: You might want to add movements and other sounds such as clapping, stomping, ripping paper, etc.

4. Follow the choral reading using Word Jazz as a writing model for students to use as a springboard for their own original kinds of Jazz.

LANGUAGE FLEXIBILITY

How many things can you name that:

Crash	Snap	Sizzle

Hiss	Hum	Groan

Plop	Pop	Sputter

SOUND & SENSE

Which is louder?

crash or plop	ping or smash
bang or blip	buzz or hum
roar or murmur	honk or zip

Which is harder?

clatter or drip   splash or crunch

Which is softer?

fizz or click   rip or squish

Which sounds could you hear in the city?

beep boom caw croak roar squeal honk bong cluck

Which sounds could you hear in a forest?

buzz ping rattle chirp slutter rip roar grind hiss

Which sounds could you hear in both the city and the forest?

quack splash tick twang zip cluck honk fizz rustle

LANGUAGE APPLICATION

Choose the word(s) that you think best describe the action in each of the following nursery rhymes.

Humpty Dumpty sat on the wall,
Humpty Dumpty had a great fall.
All the King's horses,
And all the King's men
Couldn't put Humpty together again.

a. clomp   b. beep   c. crash   d. zap

Jack Sprat could eat no fat,
His wife could eat no lean.
And so between them both, you see,
The licked the platter clean.

a. cluck   b. slurp   c. twang   d. snap

Hickory, dickory, dock,
The mouse ran up the clock.
The clock struck one,
The mouse ran down,
Hickory, dickory, dock.

a. bong   b. creak   c. tick-tick   d. sputter

Polly put the kettle on,
Polly put the kettle on,
Polly put the kettle on,
We'll all have some tea.

a. boing   b. whistle   c. rustle   d. blurt

WORD JAZZ

Parts: Groups A & B, Solos 1-8.

Group A:
Beep goes the horn,
Bang goes the drum,

Group B:
Bong goes the gong,
Plop goes the plum.

Group A:
Squeal spin the tires,
Smack pops my gum,

Solo 1:
Chirp goes the chick,

Solo 2:
Chug goes the train,

Group A:
Buzz goes the bee,
Splish goes the rain.

Solo 3:
Roar says the lion,

Solo 4:
Bark bays the dog,

Group B:
Screech calls the eagle,
Oink snorts the hog.

Solo 5:
Click go my dog's claws
scratching mother's floor,

Solo 6:
Rap goes my mom's knuckles
A'knocking on my door.

Group A:
Sizzle burns the sun
on a hot summer's day,

Solo 7:
Clink pop the ice cubes
tumbling out the tray.

Group A:
Splash goes the water
from my backyard pool,

Group B:
Ah! says my body
in the water that is cool.

Solo 8:
Moo mews my cow,
Hiss spits my snake,

Group A & B:
But buss goes my word jazz
Cause jazz is what I make!

STORY INTEGRATION WHOLE-LANGUAGE ACTIVITIES

Vocabulary extension / Character analysis (p. 52)

1. Copy the following on the chalkboard:

Strong Wind	Rabbit	Prince Cinco
The Stranger	Gondar	Sato
Hooits	Jidda	Singing Bird

2. Remind the students that these are characters from the folktales. Ask for other characters they remember. Use their suggestions to extend the list on the board.

3. Now pass out the activity sheet and encourage the students to complete it.

Story elaboration / Inferential thinking (p. 53)

Prior to passing out the activity sheet you may want to encourage the students to discuss as many of the characters as they can remember from the various folktales.

Oral communication / Story elaboration

1. The students will need to be in pairs for this activity. You will also need two toy telephones.

2. Each pair of students is to choose two characters from two different folktales. They are then to prepare a telephone conversation between these two characters.

3. After they have practiced their conversations, they are to take turns coming to the front of the classroom and actually using the telephones. The audience will attempt to guess the characters and their folktales.

   Important: Do not allow guessing to begin until "after" the telephone conversation is complete and the students hang up.

Vocabulary extension / Creative thinking (p. 54)

This activity sheet encourages students to list "kinds" of words they think of when they remember the various folktales they read.

They are to imagine that several of the folktales' characters have moved into a hotel (pictured on sheet). They are then asked to create dialogue coming from this hotel, using the words in the lists.

Inferential thinking (p. 55)

This activity sheet encourages the students to think about the various characters and objects from all of the folktales. They are then given an example of a FOR SALE ad from a newspaper and asked to compose one of their own. They must choose a folktale character and have their character selling something from a different folktale.

1. Before passing out this activity sheet ask the students to name characters from the folktales as you copy the names on the chalkboard.

2. Now create another list on the board as the students suggest objects or items from the folktales. You might want to begin the lists as shown here:

Characters	Objects
old farmer	wagon full of straw
King Atenas	a pebble

Pattern writing (p. 56)

This activity sheet encourages the students to increase their writing skills by following a simple pattern.

The sentence pattern will require them to integrate information from two different folktales and make predictions.

VOCABULARY EXTENSION / CHARACTER ANALYSIS / PATTERN WRITING

Choose four of the characters from the board and write them below. Now list words below each one that describe that character. For example:

Moncton
_____ _____ _____ _____ _____
   patient
_____ _____ _____ _____ _____
   loyal
_____ _____ _____ _____ _____
   kind
_____ _____ _____ _____ _____
   wise
_____ _____ _____ _____ _____

If Moncton had lived today she would probably have been a nurse in a small hospital because she was so caring towards the poor girl.

If Moncton had lived in the future she would probably have run a bed and breakfast space station because she seemed to enjoy having people come to her home.

Now you try! Use the characters on this sheet.

If_____ had lived _____ s/he would probably

have_____

because _____.

If_____ had lived _____ s/he would probably

have_____

because _____.

If_____ had lived _____ s/he would probably

have_____

because _____.

STORY ELABORATION / INFERENTIAL THINKING

Look at the first picture. How do you think it happened? You are to create a story of how it happened. But you must choose two characters, each from a different folktale, to include in your short explanation. For example:

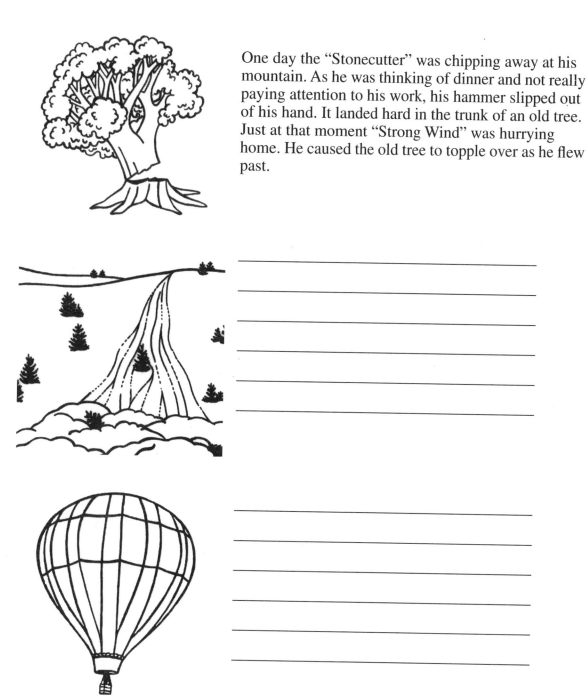

One day the "Stonecutter" was chipping away at his mountain. As he was thinking of dinner and not really paying attention to his work, his hammer slipped out of his hand. It landed hard in the trunk of an old tree. Just at that moment "Strong Wind" was hurrying home. He caused the old tree to topple over as he flew past.

VOCABULARY EXTENSION / CREATIVE THINKING

Complete the following word lists. Words must somehow relate to the folktale.

Folktale Sound	Color	Action	Size	Weather
Invisible Warrior	ice blue			
Hooits Saves Day		trudged		
Stonecutter			gigantic	
Three Oranges				torrid
Secret Ingredient		splash		
Crash Is Coming		snap		
Disappearing Donkey		hiding		
The Cleverest Son		smiled		

Several of the characters from the folktales have moved into a hotel.
You are to choose your characters and then use the words from the list
to help you fill in the cartoon bubbles with dialogue.

INFERENTIAL THINKING

Choose a character from any one of the folktales. Now choose an item or object from one of the other folktales. You are to pretend that the character wants to sell this object or item. He/she is running an ad in the local newspaper's classified section. What would he/she place in the ad to make someone want to buy it? Here is an example:

FOR SALE:

A huge wagon-load of fresh straw. This fine straw is in perfect condition for cooking! Yes, cooking! Why you will be able to feed an entire village for many years with this one wagon load of straw. You see, the straw is the "secret ingredient" for making the best soup you have ever tasted. Only one piece of straw is needed for each large pot of soup. Of course, you might want to add a few other things to suit your own particular taste. We can discuss this at the time of purchase.

The entire wagon load of straw is only $99.95.

Now You Try!

FOR SALE:

PATTERN WRITING

If Strong Wind had been in "Crash Is Coming" the two squirrels probably would have thought a fire-breathing dragon was coming.

If Hooits had been in "The Cleverest Son" the farmer's room probably would have been filled up with sunlight.

Now You Try!

If _____ had been in_____

the _____ probably would_____

_____.

If _____ had been in_____

the _____ probably would_____

_____.

BIBLIOGRAPHY OF MULTICULTURAL CHILDREN'S BOOKS

Adoff, Arnold. *All the Colors of the Race*. Beech Tree, 1982.

Anderson, Bernice. *Trickster Tales from Prairie Lodgefires*. Abingdon, 1979.

Arkhurst, Joyce Cooper. *The Adventures of Spider*. Little, Brown, 1964.

Baker, Olaf. *Where the Buffaloes Begin*. Warne, 1981.

Batherman, Muriel. *Before Columbus*. Houghton Mifflin, 1981.

Baylor, Byrd. *The Desert Is Theirs*. Scribner's Sons, 1975.

Baylor, Byrd. *A God on Every Mountain Top*. Scribner's Sons, 1981.

Baylor, Byrd. *Hawk, I'm Your Brother*. Scribner, 1976.

Baylor, Byrd. *Moonsong*. Scribner's Sons, 1982.

Baylor, Byrd. *The Other Way*. Scribner's Sons, 1978.

Baylor, Byrd. *When Clay Sings*. Scribner's Sons, 1972.

Belpre, Pura. *Once in Puerto Rico*. Warne, 1973.

Berry, James. *Spiderman Anancy*. Holt, 1988.

Bierhorst, John. *Spirit Child*. Morrow, 1984.

Bierhorst, John. *A Cry from the Earth*. Four Winds, 1979.

Blackmore, Vivien. *Why the Corn is Golden*. Little, Brown, 1984.

Boholm-Olsson, Eva. *Tuan*. R & S Books, 1988.

Campbell, Barbara. *A Girl Called Bob and a Horse Called Yoki*. Dial, 1982.

Carew, Jan. *Children of the Sun*. Little, Brown, 1980.

Clark, Ann Nolan. *Secret of the Andes*. Viking, 1952.

Clark, Ann Nolan. *To Stand Against the Wind*. Viking, 1978.

Clifford, Eth. *The Remembering Box*. Beach Tree, 1985.

Clifton, Lucille. *Lucky Stone*. Delacorte, 1979.

Coatsworth, Emerson. *The Adventures of Nanabush*. Atheneum, 1980.

Coerr, Eleanor. *Mieko and the Fifth Treasure*. Putnam, 1993.

Coerr, Eleanor. *Sadako and the Thousand Paper Cranes*. Dell, 1977.

Conger, David. *Many Lands, Many Stories*. Tuttle, 1987.

Courlander, Harold. *Cow-Tall Switch and Other West African Stories*. Holt, 1947.

Courlander, Harold. *The Crest and the Hide*. Coward, McCann, 1982.

Curtis, Edward. *The Girl Who Married a Ghost*. Four Winds, 1978.

DeKay, James. *Meet Martin Luther King, Jr*. Random, 1969.

Dunn, Marylois. *The Absolutely Perfect Horse.* Harper & Row, 1983.

Ellis, Veronica. *Afro-Bets First Book About Africa.* Just Us Books, 1990.

Esbensen, Barbara. *The Star Maiden.* Little, Brown, 1988.

Estes, Eleanor. *Hundred Dresses.* Harcourt, 1944.

Ferris, Jeri. *Go Free of Die.* Carolrhoda, 1988.

Fox, Paula. *How Many Miles to Babylon?* White, 1967.

Freedman, Russell. *Buffalo Hunt.* Holiday House, 1988.

Fritz, Jean. *The Double Life of Pocahontas.* Putnam, 1983.

Garland, Sherry. *The Lotus Seed.* Harcourt Brace Jovanovich, 1993.

Goble, Paul. *Buffalo Woman.* Bradbury, 1984.

Goble, Paul. *The Girl Who Loved Wild Horses.* Bradbury, 1978.

Graham, Gail B. *The Beggar in the Blanket & Other Vietnamese Tales.* Dial, 1970.

Greenfield, Eloise. *Nathaniel Talking.* Black Butterfly Children's Books, 1989.

Greenfield, Eloise. *Paul Robeson.* Crowell, 1975.

Greenfield, Eloise. *Rosa Parks.* Crowell, 1973.

Greenfield, Eloise. *Sister.* Crowell, 1974.

Greenfield, Eloise. *Under the Sunday Tree.* Harper & Row, 1988.

Griego y Maestas, Jose. *Cuentos: Tales from the Hispanic Southwest.* Museum of New Mexico, 1980.

Hall, Lynn. Danza! Scribner's Sons, 1981.

Hamilton, Virginia. The Bells of Christmas. Harcourt Brace Jovanovich, 1989.

Hamilton, Virginia. Zeely. Macmillan, 1967.

Hamilton, Virginia. M. C. Higgins, The Great. Macmillan, 1974.

Hamilton, Virginia. The People Could Fly. Knopf, 1985.

Hargreaves, Pat. *The Caribbean and Gulf of Mexico.* Silver Burdett, 1980.

Harris, Joel Chandler. *Jump! The Adventures of Brer Rabbit.* Harcourt Brace Jovanovich, 1986.

Harris, Joel Chandler. *Jump Again! More Adventures of Brer Rabbit.* Harcourt Brace Jovanovich, 1987.

Haviland, Virginia. *North American Legends.* Philomel, 1979.

Hinojosa, Francisco. *The Old Lady Who Ate People.* Little, Brown, 1984.

Holling, Holling C. *Paddle-to-the-Sea.* Houghton Mifflin, 1949.

Jagendorf, M. A. *The King of the Mountains.* Vanguard, 1960.

Jaquith, Priscilla. *Bo Rabbit Smart for True.* Philomel, 1981.

Kimmel, Eric. *Hershel and the Hanukkah Goblins.* Holiday House, 1989.

Kroll, Virginia. *Africa Brother and Sisters.* Four Winds Press, 1993.

Kurtycz, Marcos. *Tigers and Opossums: Animal Legends.* Little, Brown, 1984.

Lester, Julius. *How Many Spots Does a Leopard Have?* Scholastic, 1989.

Levitin, Sonia. *Journey to America.* Atheneum, 1970.

Lindop, Edmund. *Cuba.* Watts, 1980.

Lord, Bette Bao. *In the Year of the Boar and Jackie Robinson.* Harper & Row, 1984.

Mangurian, David. *Children of the Incas.* Macmillan, 1979.

Martinello, Marian L. *With Domingo Leal in San Antonio 1734.* The University of Texas, 1979.

Mathis, Sharon Bell. *The Hundred Penny Box.* Viking, 1975.

McDermott, Gerald. *Anansi the Spider.* Holt, Reinhart & Winston, 1972.

McDermott, Gerald. *Arrow to the Sun*. Viking, 1974.

McKissack, Patricia. *Jesse Jackson*. Scholastic, 1989.

Medearis, Angela. Shelf. *Dancing With the Indians*. Holiday House, 1991.

Meltzer, Milton. *The Hispanic Americans*. Crowell, 1982.

Metayer, Maurice. *Tales from the Igloo*. Hurtig, 1972.

Mohr, Nicholasa. *Felita*. Dial, 1979.

Monjo, F. N. *The Drinking Gourd*. Harper, 1970.

Mowat, Farley. *Lost in the Barrens*. McClelland & Stewart, 1966.

Musgrove, Margaret. *Ashanti to Zulu*. Dial, 1976.

Neville, Emily. *Berries Goodman*. Harper, 1965.

Nhuong, Huynh. *The Land I Lost*. Harper & Row, 1982.

O'Dell, Scott. *Black Star, Bright Dawn*. Houghton Mifflin, 1988.

Patterson, Lillie. *Frederick Douglass: Freedom Fighter*. Garrard, 1965.

Petry, Ann. *Harriet Tubman: Conductor on the Underground Railroad*. Crowell, 1955.

Phillips, Betty Lou. *The Picture Story of Nancy Lopez*. Messner, 1980.

Rattigan, Jama Kim. *Dumpling Soup*. Little, Brown, 1993.

Robbins, Ruth. *How the First Rainbow Was Made*. Parnassus, 1980.

Roberts, Maurice. *Henry Cisneros: Mexican American Mayor*. Children's Press, 1986.

Robinson, Gail. *Raven the Trickster*. Atheneum, 1982.

Rockwood, Joyce. *Groundhog's Horse*. Holt, Rinehart & Winston, 1978.

Rohmer, Harriet. *The Invisible Hunters*. Children's Press, 1987.

Rohmer, Harriet. *Mother Scorpion Country*. Children's Press, 1987.

Rutland, Jonathan. *Take a Trip to Spain*. Watts, 1980.

Sanfield, Steve. *The Adventures of High John the Conqueror*. Watts, 1989.

Sneve, Virginia. *High Elk's Treasure*. Holiday House, 1972.

Sneve, Virginia. *Jimmy Yellow Hawk*. Holiday House, 1972.

Sneve, Virginia. *When Thunder Spoke*. Holiday House, 1974.

Speare, Elizabeth George. *Sign of the Beaver*. Houghton Mifflin, 1983.

Spencer, Paula Underwood. *Who Speaks for Wolf*. Tribe of Two Press, 1983.

Spier, Peter. *People*. Doubleday, 1980.

Stanley, Diane. *Shaka: King of the Zulus*. Morrow, 1988.

Steptoe, John. *The Story of Jumping Mouse*. Lothrop, Lee & Shepard, 1984.

Takashima, Shizuye. *Child in Prison Camp*. Tundra Books, 1971.

Taylor, Mildred. *The Gold Cadillac*. Dial, 1987.

Taylor, Sidney. *All-Of-A-Kind Family*. Follett, 1951.

Taylor, Sidney. *All-Of-A-Kind Family Uptown*. Follett, 1958.

Toye, William. *The Loon's Necklace*. Oxford, 1977.

Turner, Glennette Tilley. *Take a Walk in Their Shoes*. Cobblehill Books, 1989.

Wagner, Jane, Dell. *J. T.* 1969.

Wallas, James. *Kwakiutl Legends*. Hancock House, 1981.

Walter, Mildred Pitts. *Justin and the Best Biscuits in the World*. Lothrop Lee & Shepard, 1986.

Weik, Mary Hays. *The Jazz Man*. Atheneum, 1966.

White, Clarence. *Cesar Chavez, Man of Courage*. Garrard, 1973.

White Deer of Autumn. *Ceremony—In the Circle of Life.* Raintree, 1983.

Yagawa, Sumiko. *The Crane Wife.* Morrow, 1981.

Yee, Paul. *Tales from Gold Mountain.* Macmillan, 1990.

Yep, Lawrence. *The Rainbow People.* Harper & Row, 1989.